Human A Different Way

Pocket Guide to

Problem Solving

Elemental Publishing
Monroe, WA

Website: HumanADifferentWay.com
ISBN: 978-1-7320763-4-1
© 2023 Boston Carter

All rights reserved. No portion of this book shall be copied, scanned, electronically stored, or shared in any way without express written permission from the publisher. Portions of up to 100 words of this book may be quoted without permission provided that those quotes are represented according to their context.

Table of Contents

Philosophical Foundations	—1
Our Approach	—7
Breathing	—9
Awareness	—13
Listening	—15
Synchronicity	—16
Archetypal Symbolism	—19
Active Imagination	—21
Sudden Thoughts or Feelings	—29
Use of Will	—35
Wake to a Solution	—37
Application	—39
Personal Problems	—43
Closing	—47

Human A Different Way

Pocket Guide to Problem Solving

Boston Carter, Ph.D.
with
Katherine Baxter

Gordon Johnson from Pixabay

Philosophical Foundations

Once considered the domain of the esoteric spiritual adept, the higher-self is now being realized as a vastly underutilized and misunderstood facet of the human psyche. A part of the psyche that everyone is familiar with is the instincts, although it isn't commonly referred to that way. When I say instinct, I mean a manner in which the psyche functions to provide a way of seeing the world. Instinct is an imprint upon the mind that occurs at birth. Most people have an understanding of this in animals, but not so much in ourselves. What human instinct does is provide a means to survive. It does this by creating a linear, two-dimensional pattern of perception. In other words, we all are born seeing the world through a specific patterned lens. There are four lenses and each one carries different attributes of perception. What all four have in common is that they are linear and binary This means that the instinctive process reduces decisions to a two option choice. In the alphabet of decision making, what this does is reduce options and choices to the simplest formula. Instinct takes you from A to Z without taking the time to look at all the letters in between Why? Because limiting our options allows for fast decision making, which is needed in survival situations. It has served humans well as the species evolved. It's a lot easier, and faster, to decide between fight or flight than it is to consider negotiating, listening, or any number of other options when in survival mode. Instinct protects us by limiting our thinking in this way. However, when survival of the individual compromises survival of the collective, this two-dimensional approach can cause more problems that it solves. Survival mode means competition for resources. A sense of competition and desire for power is embedded in the instinctual patterns of perception, each of which is driven by a fear of loss, or not having enough. In a complex and sophisticated society, the ultimate survival of the collective requires cooperation and collaboration. The old thinking of the instinct no longer serves to protect the species as a whole.

You might say, "ok, but I'm not in a survival situation so why are we talking about this?" Because instincts are also the default perception for the human psyche. Instincts are based in fear, which translates as competition, power, self-centeredness, etc. Solving problems from these attributes of perception only causes more problems. You can't create a compassionate, cooperative world from instincts. It simply isn't possible. With a global population of eight billion people, solving collective problems from instincts isn't feasible. There is nowhere to flee and there are too many power struggles. In a world at the breaking point in so many ways, the old thinking no longer serves and humanity must reach for a transcendent function to adapt. There is another part of us that perceives through compassion, equity, and cooperation. That part is called higher self. Finding solutions from that perspective helps the whole collective. We can no longer function with a winner takes all, me first paradigm. The only way for one of us to thrive is for all of us to thrive by working together. That is the reality with which we are faced.

Our planet is very far away from any known sources of aid. We are alone here and it is up to us to solve the problems that we have created through the instinct perceptions. We must move our awareness into a compassionate, loving perspective of problem solving. Human A Different Way is about learning how to access higher self and utilize it to solve problems so that all people, animals, and planet can thrive. We are building a community of people that want a New World that begins with a New America, a New State, New Neighborhood, family and self.

There is a difference between instinct and intuition. These terms are often used interchangeably, but we would be better served to sort them out. Instinct is an imprint on the psyche that drives us to make decisions based on two-dimensional thinking. Intuition taps into the energy of consciousness of which we are typically unaware, the unconscious. However, the typically unconscious contents can be made conscious through specific practices. We adopt and utilize these practices to help us access solutions held by the wisdom of higher self, which has historically been unconscious because we thought that our instinct patterns of perception are all there is to us. Now we know better.

With the mapping of our instinct

patterns (available at humanadifferentway.com), it is now easy to see what the instinct perceptions are getting up to and how to side-step them into a stronger relationship with higher self, the place of solving problems from wisdom.

I will show you how to approach problem solving through your higher wisdom. That means learning the difference between instinct and higher self, and learning how higher self perceives, and communicates.

Our Approach

The Human A Different Way approach to problem solving involves accessing the wisdom of higher self. "Listening" to higher self is naturally available to everyone, but it is a skill that must be developed because it has to be chosen. Accessing it is not automatic like instinct is. Higher self is the complete opposite of instinct in almost every way. For that reason, relating to it may seem quite foreign in the beginning. Most mystics and intuitive practitioners are more familiar with the process and there may be different processes than those that I show you. I will share with you what I've worked out as the easiest approach that seems the most compatible, for most people, based on my experience.

Breathing

Before you can reach higher self wisdom, you have to get the instinct mind to settle down. If the instinct feels any threat or fear to any degree, it won't allow you to reach higher self. The trick to slowing instinct down, calming the nervous system, is breathing techniques. There are many forms to choose from and I will guide you through one Yoga method that is believed to calm the Vagus nerve. Please consider trying some other breathing techniques as well to see if one works better for you and this intended purpose.

You know how when you're at the dentist and you constrict your throat and tongue to block water from running down your throat while breathing through your nose? This is similar. Using your pulse rate to set the pace, take a gentle 6 count breath in through your mouth. Constrict the muscles in your throat and tongue to breathe out through your nose so that the exhaling air makes a sound like white noise. Do this for the same 6 counts. Repeat for a few breaths, until you feel relaxed and settled.

Offering a personal anecdote: when I was about 21 years old, I trained myself to breathe this way and used the white noise sound as a trigger to put myself to sleep. Doing this I could fall asleep within two minutes, which I did because I wanted to set an alarm to wake me up at the end of an REM cycle to track my dreams. It worked well. Too well. I was sitting in a college class and a man behind me was breathing and making this sound. My eyes rolled up into my head as my chin fell into my chest. The instructor smiled at me as I startled awake again. This went on for the whole class. I stopped using this method of breathing as a sleep trigger. But it works great for slowing the instinct mind.

Awareness

Let me share a way that awareness can be shifted toward higher self. One is to focus on being heart-centered and another is to focus on being present with an empty mind. Both ways accomplish the same thing in that both orient your awareness to the present, a sense of peace, and a silent receptivity. I'll talk about heart-centering first.

Heart-centering is to place your awareness fully within the center of your heart chakra. To find that location, place your index finger at the base of your throat where your two collar bones meet. Then four finger-widths down and 2 inches, or 5cm, inside of your chest. Hold your attention on this spot for as long as you can manage it. What do you feel? Write about your experience of it. Chances are that if you hold your attention there, you are also present. It is difficult to be heart-centered and thinking about the past or the future at the same time.

Concentration within your heart-center requires willpower. This is how you can use your free-will to its best purpose, by staying focused on the present moment. Doing so creates a space for your awareness to hear higher self. When the instinct mind is busy making noise with thoughts of the past or the future, higher self cannot be heard because your mind is occupied. Instinct is loud, while higher self is very quiet.

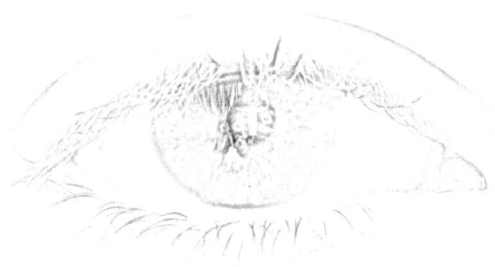

Susanne Jutzeler Schwein from Pixabay

Listening

I just told you that awareness of higher self allows it to be heard and I told you one way of making space to listen for it. The act of actually listening to higher self happens through several common avenues. Assume that all of these require your attention in the present.

- Synchronicity
- Archetypal symbolism
- Active Imagination
- Sudden thoughts/feelings
- Use of will (discipline) to seek solutions
- Ask the unconscious to work on it over night and wake up to a solution

Synchronicity

Synchronicity is a term coined by Dr. Carl Jung and it means to extract meaning from what might otherwise be seen as a coincidence that has no apparent cause. For example, I once had a spider move down its silk right in front of my face. Not in itself unusual, but not something that happens commonly either. Not an hour later it happened again in a completely different location. Given the odds of this occurrence happening twice in an hour, I think it warrants my attention as symbolic in some way. My ability to see it as symbolic, or meaningful, is what makes it a synchronicity.

Once I recognize this coincidence as a synchronicity, I begin to ask the question, "what is this about"? I turn to the folklore of spiders. Why? Because folklore, fairy tales, and stories are symbols of psychological processes. The unconscious part of the psyche emerges into the realm of awareness as symbols and images, especially through stories.

I had two spiders hanging from silk right in front of my face, as if I needed to see something about spiders that might pertain to my current circumstances. Spiders are known to weave webs. They are also known to be venomous. Native Americans use the web symbols as a dreamcatcher. What might be right in front of my face that I am not seeing? I don't know for sure, but I can go into an active imagination exercise and ask for a guide to show me what I need to know about this spider synchronicity because it now has my attention. Job well done.

Archetypal Symbolism

Archetypes are images, which can be personified, or characteristic as images, patterns, thoughts, feelings, smells, tastes, and so on. For example the God image is often personified as a gray-haired man in the sky, but has also been a burning bush (Moses). The God image is thought of as an energy that is everywhere in all things, yet is envisioned as a man or bush because that is an image that we can interpret, not because God actually looks like that. Higher self has to use what we know to communicate with us.

Archetypes are common to all people regardless of race, region, or religion because they come from the collective unconscious. Examples of archetypes are mother, father, day, night, time, joker, magician, etc. Your higher self will communicate with you in ways that you best understand using archetypal, or symbolic, images. If you will understand God as a gray-haired man, then that is the image you will see in your active imaginations. If you see God as a tree, then that is how it will appear to you. This is energy from the multi-dimensional realm, not physical reality. Your higher self will communicate with you through a language and knowledge base that you can understand. This means that images and information come to you through your own knowledge or belief system. The more you know, the easier it is for higher self to communicate with you because you provide a basis for that communication to take place.

Gordon Johnson from Pixabay

The Ouroboros is an ancient archetypal symbol of perpetual cycles and patterns of return.

Active Imagination

An active imagination exercise is a combination of asking for information and then welcoming whatever comes into the mind. There can be a fine line between striving for the answer you want (instinct), and being open to whatever shows up. I highly recommend being open to whatever shows up. I actually love when I get completely unanticipated answers because that means it did not come from my instinct mind. Instinct likes to take over whenever possible, which is why we have to stay open and not allow it to strive for its own agenda. Remain neutral.

I will give you an active imagination that will create a space for you to communicate with higher self. You may want to read out loud and record this writing so you can follow it with your eyes closed. I find it difficult to do an active imagination with my eyes open. The audio recording of this in my voice is available in our online courses at HumanADifferentWay.com.

We will imaginatively manufacture a space for that communication to take place, but then allow higher self to emerge images and feelings for us to receive. It is important not to contrive a message from higher self. Remaining heart-centered is the best way to prevent the ego/instinct from devising an outcome. Ego/instinct energies feel different than do higher self energies. Also, if you are imagining a message and you can feel energy centered in your solar plexus, that is your ego/instinct talking. If you can feel energy in your heart center, then that is higher self talking. When images occur that make no sense, it is usually because they are not part of your current reality. Higher self is speaking a language you may not have a reference for. When that happens, the information is absolutely pure. You can't concoct something that you have no knowledge of. We can design the space for communication, but not the communication itself. Please be aware that the space you create for this communication is private. No one but you and your ethereal beings are allowed in this space.

Your space can be inside or outside. It will need to have a pathway or hallway leading to it, a door or gate, a place to sit, and a screen or wall that you can see to view images. Take a moment to decide how you want your space to look. If you like modern clean lines, you may want a high-rise condo. If you love nature, you may want something outside. Add any elements that you like such as fire or water. Colors can matter too. It's up to you.

To begin, make yourself comfortable and close your eyes. Place your awareness in your heart center and take a deep breath in through your mouth for a 6 count. Use your pulse to set the pace. Exhale through your nose for 6 counts. Do this a few times to settle and calm your system. Heart centering helps keep instinct out of the way.

When you are ready, imagine that you are standing up taking a firmly planted step on the floor or ground. Take another step planting your foot firmly. Continue walking solidly on your feet. You want to be well grounded before reaching the entrance to your space. Keep walking. Just in front of you, and to your left, see a gate or door that you must pass through. Approach it and turn left to meet it. Open the door or gate and step inside your space. Close the door firmly behind you. Give the intention that no one but you ever find this entrance and it is keyed to your energy system so no one else can enter. This is a secret place. Enter the space and find your seat. Take a look around. What is here? Where do you want your large screen to be? Take another breath.

Look at your screen. What shape or image will represent your neutrality? Ask for an image that shows you when you are neutral, or unbiased in any way. Allow it to emerge on the screen. Give it as much time as you need. There is no rush. See it on the screen.

Ask your shape, or image, to make a motion that represents a neutral unbiased state of mind that is detached from outcomes. Then ask it to make a motion that represents when you are not neutral. Keep this image in the corner of your mind as you ask questions of higher self. This image you can keep with you in your daily interactions with others too so you can communicate more effectively with others by remaining neutral and unbiased. This shape or image is 100% yours.

Create a seat to your left for your higher self to sit with you. Invite it to join you in this space. How does it present to you? In what image? It may be a characteristic image rather than a personified one. However it shows up is good. What does it say to you? Spend some time sitting with it. Talking isn't necessary. Spending time with them is enough sometimes. Take a breath.

Stay in this space as long as you like. It is always here for you. You can ask higher self, "what do I most need to know"? Oftentimes, it may be that you only need a hug, or comfort from higher self. You may find this to be the case when you feel stressed. Stress is not conducive to clear communication with higher self, so it provides comfort. They offer love. You will see on your screen what they want you to know.

When you feel complete, thank your higher self for spending time with you. Watch them return to their dimension. Stand up and begin to walk back to your door or gate. Open it and pass through, closing it firmly behind you. Give the intention that it remains hidden from others under protection. Walk back up the pathway or hallway until you return to the point at which you began. Open your eyes and take a breath. Write about your experience, draw your neutrality image and take any notes that you need to about what occurred in your space. You may want to keep a journal for all of your adventures into your space. Whatever you feel about it matters.

Sudden Thoughts or Feelings

Sudden thoughts and feelings can be messages from higher self. Once upon a time, I had some synchronicities that were followed by sudden thoughts and feelings. I'll tell you about it because it was a significant message for me. I had been working at a psychic fair and there was a new person in the room selling wares from a new bookstore in another city not too far away. I didn't think much of it but several people told me about it and what a great store it was. I was busy so their comments floated by. The next week, I was riding with a friend to a holistic chamber of commerce meeting and she said, "have you been to that new bookstore? I think you should go." I said no I hadn't and we carried on to something else. When we arrived at the meeting, another person I know came up to me and said, "I want to give you this card for a new bookstore. I have a feeling that you need to check it out?" I thanked her for the card. This is just too many mentions in a short period of time for me to ignore. I begin to see this as a synchronicity and I am curious about it. But not curious enough to run right over to the bookstore. A couple of days later I was at home working on my computer and I had the sudden thought that I needed to go to that bookstore. Then I had a super strong feeling that it had to be right now. I listened and immediately left for the bookstore.

I walked in the door with a book in hand that I had written. As I spoke with the man behind the counter, I had a feeling that I'd had before. I recognized it as a karmic interaction. There was something going on here. The bookstore is a spiritual bookstore and coffeehouse. It just opened a few months prior. I talked to the man about my book and he agreed to place it on the shelf and he invited me to give a talk on the book. I agreed. Then I asked if he had space and interest to have a medical intuitive do readings for people in the store. He said yes and that I could have Saturdays.

The next Saturday I showed up and it turns out that his wife worked the store on Saturdays. She had another full time job, but worked Saturdays to give him time off. We got to know each other. The karmic, or dharmic, connection was with his wife in a big way. She became my wife fairly shortly after we met. She still is my wife 14 years later as of this writing. We all get along very well and have no hard feelings. Life happens. It was handled honestly, openly, and fairly. No secrets and no lies. What is important for you, dear reader, is that there is no other place that she and I would have met. Our paths did not cross anywhere else. That bookstore was not open for very long either so had I delayed and not listened to the thoughts and feelings that were presented, I may have missed it and lost out on the best thing that ever happened to me. It also was important to recognize the synchronicity that preceded it. Without the synchronicity, I would not have understood the thoughts and feelings.

I've experienced other situations in which I had a sudden thought about a person that I hadn't thought about. Sometimes it recurs almost like nagging. That is when I know that I need to call them. They may need my help or maybe they have something to tell me? If I feel like I need to go on a trip somewhere, I go. This is how we follow our path and inner guidance. Don't question it. If you are heart-centered and the ego/instinct is clearly not trying to derive an outcome to soothe itself, then the action should be taken.

Use of Will

Because instinct is domineering, loud, likes control, and is the default mind, higher self is the complete opposite, which is quiet, patient, waiting, and awareness of it must be chosen. Learning the difference between the two parts is necessary for recognition and awareness of higher self. It will not shout at you. It is subtle like a whisper. This is how free will comes into play. If you use your will to listen to higher self, it will guide you through life in a way that never misdirects. Instinct can misdirect simply because it seeks immediate gratification seeking any solution to soothe its insecurity. Also because it limits solutions with its two dimensional thinking. Higher self brings wisdom from a multidimensional perspective, but only if you willfully access it.

HumanADifferentWay

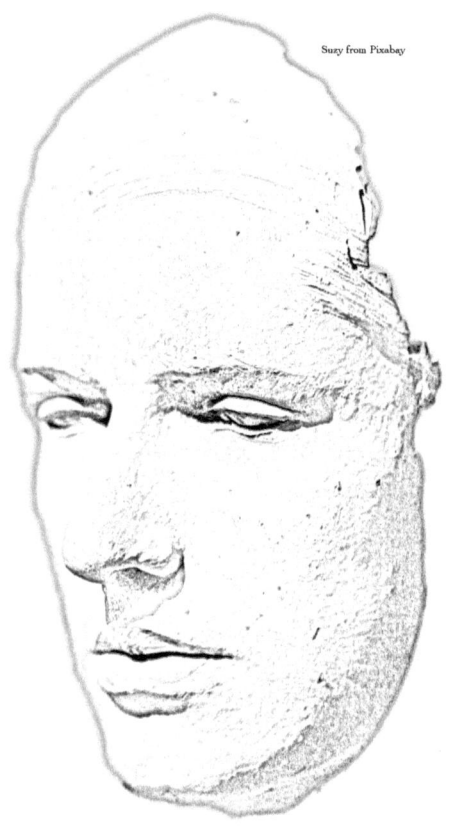

Suzy from Pixabay

Wake to a Solution

Part of your skill as a human being is to give instructions to parts of yourself. Higher self must be asked, but your innate, which is part of your biology, can be instructed. One way in which I utilize higher self is I ask higher self to show me a solution through my unconscious mind. Then I instruct my biology to work with my higher self and allow me to wake up in the morning with the solution in mind. This is using my will to get different parts of me to work together. My biology needs to work with my unconscious mind so higher self can provide a message. I can't say that I know exactly how it works, because I don't, but it works.

Sometimes it takes days or weeks for the answer to arrive. When I wrote my first book on the instinct patterns back in 2003, I struggled with how to create a diagnostic tool for people to discern which pattern is theirs. I asked for an answer to come to me. It took two months, but I did finally wake up one morning with a complete understanding of how to do it. I spent two hours writing it out and it was done. It goes that way sometimes. It's as if the psyche has to prepare to receive the information, or it has to be structured in some way. Different pieces of the puzzle don't always show up together and they have to be found. Be patient with yourself as you practice this listening. It will build and grow as you use it, and your confidence in its legitimacy will build as you see it working in your life.

Application

In what ways can these techniques of listening to higher self be used to better our lives and our world? The simple answer is every way. Communicating with higher self is central to a thriving existence. Higher self has a very different perspective than our instinct self does and consequently has solutions that we may not consider in our everyday life in which instinct most often dominates our thinking.

The ego/instinct contrives solutions based on its perspective of survival. Consequently outcomes are not as favorable. For a simple example, I use my innate, or intuitive, self to help with mundane tasks. One such task is cooking. When I put something in the oven or leave it cooking on the stovetop, I instruct my innate self to let me know when it is done. I will then go about my business paying no attention to the time. Using a timer, food doesn't turn out quite as good. As I am busy doing something else and not thinking about the food at all, I have a sudden thought that it is time to take the food off the stove or out of the oven. Then I know I have to go do it right then. If I delay at all, it won't be good. It turns out perfect every time, much better than it would with a timer.

Higher self can be utilized for problem solving in similar ways. One thing I do often is sit quietly, without distractions, and let my higher self know that I will remain sitting until I have an answer or solution. Then the challenge is to maintain focus on the heart center and keep a clear mind so I can hear or see whatever message is being sent. Answers often come in the form of a sudden thought that seems out of place, or an imaginal vision of some kind. As an example of an imaginal vision, I once wondered if I should contact someone about a specific idea. I was concerned that I might push their boundaries by doing so. The answer came in the form of a vision of the person gesturing for me to come closer. I called and it worked out well. The timing was good. Sometimes a solution is all about timing.

Gerd Altmann from Pixabay

HumanADifferentWay

Natálie Šteyerová from Pixabay

Personal Problems

The I-Ching claims that there are three ways to manage a problem:
- Try to force an outcome
- Abandon it altogether
- Allow it to work out as it will

Let's look at what each of these concepts might look like. For example, what if you want to buy a house. You've been looking and looking, but what you find is either not worth having due to ill repair, or you can't afford the asking price. After several months of searching for the right house, you find one that you want, is in a good location, and you can afford it. Someone else found it too and now it's up to the owner to decide who gets the house.

How might you go about forcing an outcome? You could pester your realtor with daily calls to see if you got it. You could search public records to find the owner and beg them to sell it to you. Maybe you could write them a sob story letter to pull on their heart strings. There are a plethora of ways in which you could try to force a favorable outcome. The problem is that you don't know if any of them would backfire. The owner may not appreciate your tactics and sell to your competitor. Your realtor will certainly notify you if you are selected so calling them every day isn't going to make it go faster or more favorably, but it could make them not want to be helpful to you. Forcing an outcome is what the ego/instinct does out of fear of not getting what it wants. Sometimes it works, but you have to be able to like yourself when you're done or the price you pay is very high indeed.

What about abandonment? In the case of this house, you could choose to withdraw your offer and let your competitor take it because you can't stand the anxiety of not having control of the situation. You could walk away and continue looking for another house that might not have a competitor. What are the chances that if you find a house that you can afford, and is in reasonable condition, that it won't have another offer? It's a risky move, but it could work. Of course you may cause yourself even more stress and anxiety by starting the process all over again.

Allowing the situation to work out on its own means to put your best foot forward and detach from outcomes. Keep your energy neutral and trust that all will go the way it should. Your ego/instinct mind does not know enough to force outcomes. It could be that after forcing, or manipulating, the purchase of your house, that the market drops and your house is now worth less than you paid for it and your interest rate is higher than it would have been had you waited.

Abandoning the situation could leave you out of a good deal. Perhaps if you had stayed in

move through our galaxy. We either change into new patterns, or we leave the planet too. Why? Because old energy and new energy oppose each other. They don't mix. Being one while living in the other leads to disease and death. Old systems are dying. We witness this in the news as a battle between left and right. Left and right are new and old. This is the reality with which we are faced and the time has come to change our systems. We have no choice about it, but it is a good thing, in my view. These changes lead us into a time of compassion, cooperation, and peace. I'm all for it even if the road to get there seems a bit bumpy. The new cannot replace the old until the old is gone. We are witnessing the old going away. That is all this is. I like to prepare and plan ahead. So the time is now to approach problem solving and create new energy systems.

Problem Solving Guide

Namaste

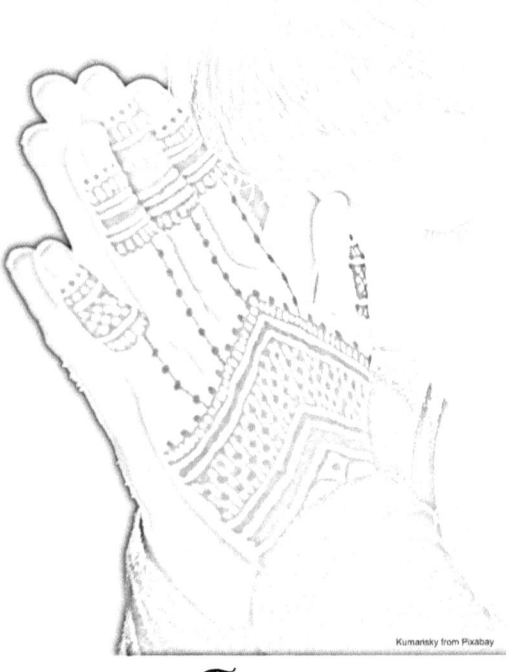

www.ingramcontent.com/pod-product-compliance
Lightning Source LLC
Chambersburg PA
CBHW060413080526
44583CB00012B/550